THE GREAT WESTERN SOCIETY

The Great Western Railway became a national institution in over a century of existence. It was promoted by the merchants of Bristol to connect their city with London and in 1833 they appointed Isambard Kingdom Brunel as engineer. The Act of Incorporation of the Great Western Railway received the Royal Assent in 1835 and Brunel started construction of the line. He was a flamboyant genius who was determined that his railway would be the finest in the land: it would have the fastest trains so he adopted a broad gauge of seven feet between the rails and he designed and built bridges, viaducts and stations on a grand scale. The soundness of his engineering means that today, although the broad gauge has long disappeared, trains speed over a virtually unchanged railway at 125mph.

In the 1930s the Great Western was very conscious of the benefits of publicity and there appeared a prodigious amount of books, jigsaw puzzles and other propaganda which ensured that the names of its locomotives such as *King George V* and *Caerphilly Castle* were household names. It was the holiday line par excellence carrying thousands of holidaymakers to west country resorts in trains of chocolate and cream carriages pulled by brunswick green steam locomotives with copper capped chimneys and sparkling brasswork. In stark contrast lengthy trains of coal trucks formed a continuous procession down the South Wales valleys carrying coal for industry and export whilst from Cheshire to Cornwall and Middlesex to Merioneth there were the rural branch-lines whose trains of one or two carriages were part of the little communities they served.

The old company became a reluctant part of the nationalised British Railways on 31st December 1947 but for a while little changed. However the modernisation of the

The engine that started it all – No. 1466 outside the engine shed at Didcot Railway Centre.

railways and the ruthless closure of branch-lines meant that by the early sixties there were dramatic changes. Diesel locomotives replaced steam, stations and signalling were rationalised and it began to be realised that in a short space of time the whole railway scene would be transformed. The sidings at Swindon Works contained more locomotives for scrapping than they had since the broad gauge was finally abolished in 1892. British Railways had announced a list of locomotives that would be retained for preservation in its museums but this was of necessity very selective. Four schoolboys, train spotting on the footbridge at Southall which overlooks the engine shed there, decided one day in 1961 that a Great Western 'push & pull' or autotrain ought to be preserved and that if no one else would do it they would try. Railway preservation was very much in its infancy at this time but a number of schemes was being floated. A letter was despatched to the 'Railway Magazine' which duly appeared in print some months later; much to everyone's surprise money started rolling in and it was necessary to put the embryo scheme on a proper footing. Thus was born the Great Western Society which in 1964 purchased locomotive No.1466 and trailer coach No.231. However it did not stop there and there was soon pressure to buy more locomotives before steam trains finally disappeared. Soon it became obvious that it was

necessary to have somewhere to keep them and the Society was offered the use of the engine shed at Didcot which had been declared redundant.

The Society moved in with three locomotives and a number of carriages in 1967 and since then the area has been transformed into Didcot Railway Centre. The aim has been to keep as much as possible of the engine shed in its original condition whilst adapting it to its present role. In the old days engine sheds were dirty places which were not open to visitors; nowadays we endeavour to keep ours as clean as is possible in an environment of coal burning steam locomotives. The exhibits and facilities such as the branch-line with its stations and signalboxes, the broad gauge demonstration, museum, locomotive and carriage works have been developed by the Great Western Society and its members who give up their spare time and money to keep alive for future generations just a small part of the Great Western Railway.

Our activities have been recognised within the railway preservation movement, gaining the Association of Independent Railway Preservation Societies award for outstanding achievements in 1975 and again in 1981, other major awards for Didcot Halt and the signalling project, a previous edition of this Guidebook was judged the best of its kind in 1990 whilst the restoration and operation of the Travelling Post Office gained the top prize in the Scania Transport trust Awards in 1997.

In the thirty years since the Society's arrival at Didcot we (and the other railway preservation groups) have learnt that there is a lot more to the operation of steam trains than their purchase and the locomotive and carriage works have been built to conserve the exhibits but the cost of restoration and repair is growing as the vehicles get older and more parts need replacing. Whilst the income from visitors' admissions and contributions from the shop and refreshment room pays for the day to day operation and maintenance of the Centre and its facilities, we depend on the support of our members for its development and long term future. Although we have a small team of full time paid administrative and some part time staff, nearly everyone associated with the Centre's operation of the Centre is a volunteer member of the Society. If you would like to help us in our work you can find a membership form in the centre of this Guide.

THE GREAT WESTERN RAILWAY AT DIDCOT

Didcot lies on the original main line of the Great Western Railway designed by Brunel. On 1st June 1840 the section through Didcot was opened and the whole route from Paddington to Bristol was completed on 30th June 1841. The line passed ten miles south of Oxford and for the first four years passengers for that city left the train at Steventon, some three miles west of Didcot. On 12th June 1844 a branch line to Oxford was opened from Didcot where a station was constructed at the junction. Didcot was then just a small village but with the coming of the railway it grew in size and importance.

In 1852 the Oxford branch was extended through to Birmingham and the Great Western came into contact with other railways built to the standard gauge of 4ft 8½. At that time the broad gauge Great Western ran the fastest trains in the country but in the interests of standardisation Parliament decreed that future railways should be built to the 4ft 8½ gauge. Thus the line to Birmingham had mixed standard and broad gauge rails and Didcot became an important junction where goods and passengers for the West of England were transferred from one train to another. The need to transfer traffic at places like Didcot caused considerable delay and expense and the GWR gradually converted its lines to mixed gauge until by the time the broad gauge was finally abolished in 1892 the only broad gauge trains at Didcot were through express and goods trains to the west of England.

In 1882 the Great Western monopoly at Didcot was

The railway scene at Didcot over one hundred years ago with a westbound broad gauge express.

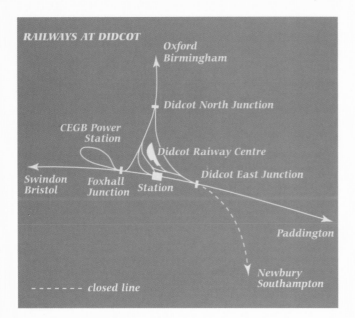

RAILWAYS AT DIDCOT

Oxford
Birmingham

Didcot North Junction

CEGB Power
Station

Didcot Railway Centre

Swindon
Bristol

Foxhall
Junction

Station

Didcot East Junction

Paddington

Newbury
Southampton

- - - - - - - closed line

operates Inter City 125 High Speed Trains on the Paddington-Bristol route whilst the Birmingham line is served by Cross Country trains and local services to Oxford and the Thames Valley are provided by Thames Trains. There is considerable commuter traffic to London and the closure of wayside stations means that Didcot is now the railhead for Wantage and Abingdon; in 1985 the station was rebuilt, a large new carpark provided where the GWR provender store once stood, and renamed Didcot Parkway to acknowledge its new role. The freight yard continues to be active to the extent that a new diesel locomotive fuelling point was built in 1994. Didcot Power Station, a landmark that can be seen from miles around, attracts a constant flow of 'merry-go-round' coal trains though that will change when the new gas fired station is completed.

broken with the opening of the Didcot, Newbury & Southampton Railway which headed south across the sparsely populated Berkshire Downs. Although its trains were always operated by the GWR it remained an independent company until 1923.

A small engine shed had been built at Didcot in 1844 and this was replaced by a larger building in 1857 but by the early years of the 20th century it too was inadequate. The GWR took advantage of the Loans & Guarantees Act of 1929 which provided funds to relieve unemployment during the depressed years of the twenties and thirties to build a completely new depot in 1932, at the same time reconstructing the passenger station. It is this depot which is now the focal point of Didcot Railway Centre. The closure in the 1960s of the Didcot, Newbury & Southampton line, the nearby Milton Ordnance Depot and Moreton Cutting sidings together with dieselisation made the depot redundant and it was officially closed to steam on 14th June 1965 although it was still used for stabling diesel locomotives until December 1969.

Nevertheless Didcot is still an important centre for both passenger and freight traffic. The proud name of Great Western has been revived for the new private company which

The engine shed at Didcot as seen from the coaling stage in the early 1960s.

A GUIDED TOUR

The Didcot Railway Centre is reached through the subway which runs below Didcot Parkway Station. As part of our country's privatised railway, the station, signalling and trackwork is now owned by Railtrack plc.

As you climb the steps from the subway, you are entering a bygone era, just as the Great Western railwaymen did when they reported for duty at the engine shed. You cross the shunting lines (now derelict) via a board crossing to the gates of the Didcot Railway Centre, home of the Great Western Society. To your right, you will see the hut bearing the plate "Didcot Ground Frame" which was originally used to control points in the sidings by Didcot station. The Society moved it to its current location and it is now used a as a booking office to sell and check admission tickets.

Just take a moment and look around! You are entering the Centre at its eastern or London end. To your right are the double gates giving the Society access to the rail network for bringing in supplies such as coal, spare parts, etc. and for the movement of locomotives engaged on railtour duties. Directly opposite is Eynsham platform, where on Steamdays, free train rides are available in our preserved GWR coaches. The Centre is completely "rail-locked" and enclosed by a chain link fence separating it from the rail network.

Beyond the fence is the Didcot East Curve and during the course of your visit, you will no doubt see CrossCountry trains on their journeys from the North and Midlands to the South Coast, Thames Trains Turbos operating the Paddington to Oxford service and maybe a freightliner or two from the North to Southampton Docks.

On a Steamday, the choice is now yours! Have a train ride straightaway or start your tour of the 16 acre site which is over half a mile long. To make access easier, particularly for visitors with wheelchairs or pushchairs, a series of footpaths has been constructed from the entrance to all major points of interest. This section of the guidebook describes the most important areas to be visited on your walk around the Centre.

Turn left from the entrance and look down towards the engine shed. You will notice that the tracks fan out through a series of points. The right hand track gives access to the main demonstration line and the middle lines serve the engine shed. To the left is the ash road and the coaling stage.

Pannier tank No. 3738 arrives at the station on the main demonstration line.
The platform is constructed from sections recovered from Eynsham on the Oxford to Fairford branch line, whilst the waiting room is a newly built building to a Great Western design.

A scene inside the engine shed during one of the annual Photographers' Evenings.

THE ASH ROADS

These are the tracks used by locomotives to allow the crews to "drop" the fire at the end of a day's work. The ash and clinker from the firebox, ashpan and smokebox door is deposited into the pit which is removed into wagons for disposal at a later date.

During the 1939-45 war, a corrugated iron shelter was built to cover the ash roads to prevent the glow of the fire's embers being seen by enemy aircraft. Unfortunately, this structure became unsafe with age and was dismantled by the Society in 1974. However, traces of it are still visible. On the embankment side of the track you will see a brick retaining wall with the remains of the steel supporting pillars in situ.

THE COALING STAGE

Behind the ash roads, a siding climbs up the embankment to the brick built coaling stage. Loaded coal wagons are propelled up the slope by a shunting locomotive and the coal is manually off loaded on to the steel floor of the coaling stage. As required, coal is then shovelled into the wheeled tubs, each containing half a ton (508 kg) of coal. Tubs are pushed on to a ramp at the front of the stage and tipped up to allow the coal to fall into either the bunker or tender of the locomotive waiting below. The Great Western Railway used soft, Welsh steam coal and this method of coaling was devised to prevent the coal being smashed to dust. Above the coaling stage sits a large tank holding 74,250 gallons (337,540 litres) of water which supplies the water cranes in front of the engine shed and various hydrants around the Centre. In Great Western days the tank was fed from a pond in the triangle of the lines to Oxford, but since the establishment of the Railway Centre the supply comes from the water main.

THE ENGINE SHED

There has been an engine shed near this site since the very early days of the Great Western Railway. In fact, the first one was constructed in 1844 when the branch line from Didcot to Oxford was first opened.

The present shed was built in 1932 and has four tracks each 200 feet (60.96 metres) long. It can accommodate three tender engines or six tank engines on each "road", to use the railway terminology. When the shed was originally opened, the allocation was around forty locomotives so not all could

The coaling stage: coal is being emptied from a tub into the tender of No. 6998 Burton Agnes Hall.

be housed at the same time. Obviously, many were out working and others were stabled on the adjacent sidings. Nowadays, it houses the Society's locomotives that have been restored and those awaiting restoration. On the left hand side of the shed is a brick lean-to building which was used for shed offices and stores. Currently around half the accommodation is used for its original purpose, whilst the rest has been adapted to house the administration offices of the Great Western Society.

In the roof are long ventilators made from plywood

which are designed to carry smoke out of the shed from locomotives in steam or in the process of being lit up. From the outside the shed you can see that the ventilators are connected to distinctive tall square chimneys.

Notice also that only three of the four "roads" have ventilators. The fourth was never replaced when British Railways reconstructed the shed roof in 1963 when steam was fast disappearing from the then Western Region of British Railways.

The small brick building in front of the shed was originally used for drying the sand used by steam locomotives to help prevent the driving wheels slipping on wet and greasy rails.

THE LIFTING SHOP

The lifting shop is located immediately behind the engine shed and is the principal workshop of the Society. In Great Western days, only minor repairs were carried out and locomotives requiring heavy overhaul were always sent to the Company's works at Swindon. The vast majority of Great Western locomotives were constructed at Swindon Works although a small number were built by outside contractors for various reasons. Nowadays, the complete restoration of a locomotive is carried out in the Lifting Shop and the Locomotive Works using machinery installed by the Great Western Society. Much of this machinery is still belt driven as it was originally installed, reflecting the engineering skills of the 1930s.

An essential part of the equipment is the Goliath overhead crane which is electrically driven and capable of lifting the largest locomotive boiler off its frames when commencing a complete overhaul.

DIDCOT LOCOMOTIVE WORKS

In the tour so far, all the buildings described were part of the 1932 Great Western depot designed to house, service and carry out minor repairs on a fleet of operational steam locomotives. Since the Great Western Society made its home at Didcot in 1967, a new role has emerged entailing the complete restoration and maintenance of the unique collection of locomotives by a volunteer workforce of Society members. It was soon realised that additional facilities were required if we were to continue with this vital role, so in 1986, the Society's 25th anniversary year, a fund was launched to build the locomotive works. With generous donations from Society members, supplemented by grants from Oxfordshire County Council and the English Tourist Board, the foundations were

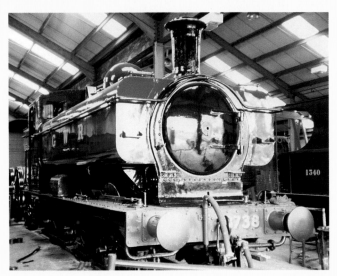

Pannier tank No. 3738 inside the Locomotive Works, awaiting the finishing touches after overhaul.

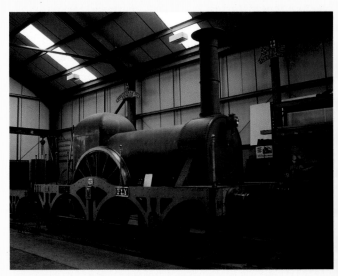

Fire Fly is a replica broad gauge locomotive that is being constructed at Didcot by the Fire Fly Project.

laid in the autumn of 1986. The building was formally commissioned in April 1988.

Due to the nature of the work involved it is not possible to allow visitors unlimited access to the works. However, there is a designated walking route through the building which is clearly marked and visitors can see at first hand the scale of the engineering work being carried out.

THE TURNTABLE

The original turntable installed on this site in 1932 was a standard 65 feet (19.812 metres) over girder of Great Western design. With the demise of steam on the Western Region of British Railways in 1965, the turntable was no longer required, so it was removed and the pit filled in. It was considered essential for the operation of the Centre to replace the turntable, as the only other method of turning locomotives was to use the Didcot triangle with the cooperation of British Rail.

After a lengthy search, a 70 feet (21.336 metres) Southern Railway example originally constructed by Ransome and Rapier Limited, was located in Southampton Docks. As this was longer than the original, not only did the pit have to be dug out, but it also had to be widened and deepened. The extra length gained has been very useful in accommodating large visiting locomotives from other railways, which in general, are longer than those of Great Western design. The sight of a locomotive being turned is a popular attraction on steam open days.

There are two methods of rotating the table, either by directly pushing the extension levers at each end of the table or by hand rotation of the gearing system located at one end. The second method is preferred when turning one of the larger locomotives.

THE CARRIAGE SHED

It is not generally appreciated that carriages, particularly the older wooden bodied ones, will deteriorate faster than locomotives if left out in the open all year. Not only are they obviously affected by cold and wet conditions, but hot sunshine can be just as detrimental. It can also cost just as much to restore a coach as a locomotive, so it becomes essential that coaches are protected before, during and after restoration.

No. 6998 Burton Agnes Hall on the Southern Railway turntable brought from Southampton Docks.

When the Great Western Society moved to Didcot, some coaches were stored in the engine shed and the remainder lived on sidings around the site. As the locomotive fleet grew, it became necessary to separate locomotives from coaches, and in 1977, the purpose built carriage shed was erected. During 1990 the shed was doubled in size enabling the vast majority of the priceless collection to be kept under cover away from the ravages of the British climate.

The shed has seven tracks or "roads". The left hand road (viewed from the front) consists of a restoration bay with raised platforms to enable work to be carried out at varying heights. The paint shop is behind the restoration bay, and behind that, a fully equipped woodworking shop which was commissioned in 1995. The next two roads are equipped for the restoration of early wooden bodied carriages and the remaining roads are used for storage of both restored and unrestored vehicles.

Visitors will note that the restoration bay is directly connected to the Centre's rail network whereas the other tracks are fed in through the traverser.

THE TRAVERSER

One line feeds into the traverser and six carriage roads lead off it. This is a great space saver and is cost effective because five sets of points and associated trackwork are not required. The principle is simple: a coach is propelled onto the traverser table by a shunting locomotive. The traverser tractor unit then moves the coach sideways until it is aligned with the appropriated shed road. The coach is then man-handled into place using pinch bars and muscle!

The Didcot traverser and tractor unit was originally built by the Midland Railway for use at its Derby Works in the 1890s. As built, it was steam driven but was converted to 400 volts d.c. electric operation with overhead pickups. It became redundant at Derby in the 1970s because the newly introduced High Speed Train mark 3 coaches were too long to fit on to it.

Electric operation at Didcot was deemed inappropriate, so the tractor unit was completely rebuilt and fitted with a Leyland Mini Metro engine and automatic transmission unit with valuable help from staff of British Leyland's Longbridge Works in Birmingham.

DIDCOT HALT AND THE BRANCH LINE

The branch line gives visitors the opportunity to enjoy a second train ride within the Centre and is operated by small tank locomotives or the ex GWR diesel railcar, creating the atmosphere of the 1930s. This enables our visitors to go back in time and experience every day rural travel of that era. Passengers join the train at Didcot Halt which was created using the same methods as employed by the Great Western Railway, and where possible, utilising buildings and fittings recovered from closed stations around the Great Western system. Construction started on the Halt in 1980 and it was opened with the branch for traffic in 1981.

As you approach the Halt, you will notice a small wooden ticket office which was recovered from Welford Park on Berkshire's Newbury to Lambourn branch. Opposite the office is the entrance to our garden which houses many interesting exhibits, many of which were recovered from local stations in Berkshire and Oxfordshire. The waiting shelter on the platform is one of the distinctive GWR "Pagoda" style, so called because of the curiously shaped roof. These corrugated iron buildings were to be found all over the Great Western system in a variety of sizes. This example came from Stockcross and Bagnor Halt, also on the Lambourn branch. One is still in daily use at Appleford Halt, which is the next station down the line to Oxford.

The fireman's eye view from the footplate of No. 1466 as it sets off from Didcot Halt for its journey along the branch line.

The lamp posts and "spear" fencing in and around the Halt area have been brought from GWR stations, and along with the buildings, have been painstakingly restored. It has taken many years to achieve the result you see today, and the efforts of the restoration team responsible were rewarded when they won a First Class Award in the Association of Railway Preservation Societies' Best Preserved Station competition. This award, in the form of a small plaque, may be viewed from the path between the Halt and Radstock North signal box.

Work on the branch line commenced in 1979 and it was opened for traffic in 1981. A ride along it is pure nostalgia: leaving the Halt, the train passes Radstock North Signal Box on your right and rumbles over the level crossing with

Radstock siding on the left. Beyond the crossing on the right is the water column which was transported from Bodmin in Cornwall, and during the course of the day, the locomotive will take on water from here. Further down the branch, the broad gauge project can be viewed on the right. Finally, Frome Mineral Junction signal box is passed on the left prior to entering the transfer shed where the train terminates. On most Steamdays, you can alight here and either walk back along the Centre or return by train. The choice is yours!

GREAT WESTERN SIGNALLING

No branch line would be complete without its signalling system. Didcot's Signal and Telegraph Department originated from a desire to preserve some of the operational elements of GWR signalling practice that made it one of the world's safest lines. GWR semaphore signals always moved down to display the "clear" position to the driver, and several of these distinctive types are positioned on the Branch operated by signal boxes at either end of the line.

Radstock North Signalbox, built around 1900 at the Reading Signal Works, was transported in kit form to Radstock and erected on site. It is a typical GWR design but has a unique feature: it was fitted with a rear window overlooking the road to enable the signalman to observe traffic before operating the crossing gates. The lever frame which controls the points and signals was also made at the Reading works in 1898. The box

Inside Radstock North signalbox showing the block instruments and part of the lever frame.

was rescued by the Society's Bristol Group in 1976, transported by low loader to Didcot, and restored to working condition, being re-commissioned in 1985. "Radstock North" is open to our visitors on major steam days when members of the S and T Department give short talks on its history and operation. Additionally, on selected days the signalbox is operated by trained signalmen to demonstrate GWR branch line signalling practice. In 1989 the signalbox won the Ian Allan Railway Heritage Award for the best restored signalbox - the first time such an award was presented.

Between Didcot Halt and Radstock Box is the pick-up and set down apparatus for the single line staff system used to control the train movements. To the right of the Box is the operational level crossing controlled by the large wheel visible inside the signalbox. The corrugated iron structure on the far side of the crossing was originally the Parcel Office at Winscombe Station on the Cheddar Valley line, but is now used by the S and T Department as a workshop. Parallel to the fence is the link line which allows rolling stock access to the branch from the site network. This line is fitted with a sand drag removed from Ashley Hill in Bristol to protect both branch and access gate. This is necessary as the site is on a falling gradient towards the north end.

Frome Mineral Junction Signalbox dates back to 1875 and was moved from Somerset to Didcot in 1983. It has been

The exterior of Radstock North signalbox.

Frome Mineral Junction signalbox; on the right is part of the overhead wire system of signal control which can also be seen in the other photographs on this page.

reconstructed and fully restored to original working condition on its present site next to the Transfer shed. The box controls the signals on the broad gauge lines by means of a unique overhead wire system designed and used by the GWR in the 1880s at major junctions such as Newton Abbot and Swindon. This system can be seen carried on the large wooden posts located beside Frome Box and adjacent to the broad gauge signals.

Other exhibits of note in this area are the early disc and

An example of an early junction signal with the arms passing through slots in the post.

The mixed gauge turnout showing the standard gauge crossing from one side to the other, with the capstan and disc & crossbar signals on the right.

crossbar signal operated by the overhead wire system and a cast iron 'capstan' signal both dating from the broad gauge era. As originally erected, these signals were operated by a railway "bobby" who allowed trains to pass at a pre-selected time interval. An example of a "bobby's box" or shelter has been reconstructed opposite the signals.

Many of the components involved in the scheme had to be made from scratch since the originals were all scrapped before the turn of the 20th Century. The S & T Department is very grateful to have received a Science Museum grant to assist with this work which was completed and commissioned during 1996; on its completion the Department won a further award from the Association of Independent Railway Preservation Societies in recognition of the high standard of historical research undertaken to create this unique project.

THE BROAD GAUGE RAILWAY

The broad gauge track is sited alongside the branch line at the northern (or Oxford) end of the Centre and a large part of the layout can be seen from the branch train. It starts just beyond the carriage shed and terminates inside the Transfer Shed.

The idea of reconstructing a broad gauge railway stemmed from the discovery by the Society's Taunton Group of a long disused siding leading to a quarry at Burlescombe, just off the GWR main line between Taunton and Tiverton. The siding, which had been lost in the undergrowth for years, had been laid at the turn of the 20th Century to standard gauge, utilising broad gauge rails and fittings made redundant after the GWR finally abandoned the broad gauge in 1892.

It was soon realised that there was sufficient equipment to create a broad gauge demonstration line which would be of significant historical importance. As further track was uncovered, the project has expanded to provide a line on which a broad gauge train can operate. In the years prior to the abolition of the broad gauge in May 1892, the GWR had been converting to mixed gauge with a third rail laid inside the broad gauge lines. This enabled standard gauge trains to use the same track and this scenario has been recreated at Didcot on the main section. Although later broad gauge tracks were laid in the modern method using normal bullhead rail on transverse sleepers, Brunel initially used a "baulk road" using bridge rails (so called because of their cross section) laid on heavy longitudinal baulks of timber. These were held apart at

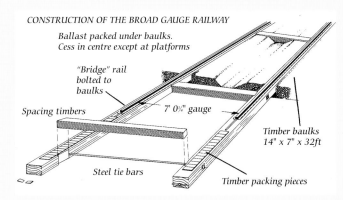

CONSTRUCTION OF THE BROAD GAUGE RAILWAY

Ballast packed under baulks. Cess in centre except at platforms

"Bridge" rail bolted to baulks

Spacing timbers

7' 0¼" gauge

Timber baulks 14" x 7" x 32ft

Steel tie bars

Timber packing pieces

The method of construction of Broad Gauge tracks using long horizontal timbers (baulks), bridge section rail and cross spacers of timber, clamped with steel rods.

the correct gauge of 7 feet 0¼ inches (2.14 metres) between the rails by means of cross timber spacers and bolted steel cross ties. Comparatively, the standard gauge is quite small at 4 feet 8½ inches (1.435 metres).

Halfway along the mixed gauge is a point or turnout which illustrates the complications caused even with a relatively simple track layout. Yet a further difficulty inherent with mixed gauge is that the inner standard gauge rail has to be opposite a station platform to ensure a standard gauge train comes alongside the platform edge to allow passenger access to the coaches. This change from one side to the other has been incorporated in the turnout.

In 1986 it was possible to run a broad gauge train in Didcot for the first time since 1892. In the early 1980s, the Science Museum commissioned the construction of a replica locomotive *Iron Duke*, a single wheeled express locomotive originally built in 1847, and two broad gauge carriages which are normally housed at the National Railway Museum in York.

Thanks to the generosity of the two museums, the train was made available to the Great Western Society for its 25th anniversary celebrations in 1986. The movement of the train to and from Didcot involved considerable difficulties and expense, but it is hoped to repeat the exercise again. Meanwhile, the "Firefly" Trust is currently constructing another broad gauge locomotive at the Centre and this may be seen in the Locomotive Works.

THE TRANSFER SHED

For many years, there was a mixture of broad and standard gauges at Didcot. The Transfer Shed, which stands at the most northerly part of our site, was originally constructed around 1863 next to the Bristol main line, west of Didcot Station, roughly where the large car park is now situated. It was dismantled and reassembled in its present location in the 1970s using Manpower Services Commission schemes sponsored by the Great Western Society.

Its current purpose is to act as a terminus for both the branch line and the broad gauge railway but its original purpose was, as the name implies, to transfer goods from one gauge to the other. At the time the shed was constructed, the GWR main line to the West and Wales was broad gauge and the line north to Oxford and Birmingham was standard gauge. The delay and disruption to goods traffic caused by such operations was the principal reason for the conversion of the broad gauge. It was a labour intensive exercise and goods were moved between wagons either manually or by using a hand operated 5 ton crane, an example of which can be seen inside the shed.

THE MAIN DEMONSTRATION LINE

Our main demonstration line used on Steamdays runs along the whole length of the Centre, parallel to the Didcot East Curve and is separated from Railtrack property by a chain link fence. Access to the line for the trains is via a link line and gate clearly visible from the path as you walk along the Centre.

Passengers join the train at a platform opposite the entrance to the Centre. This rather austere structure, made up of concrete sections, was originally erected by the GWR at Eynsham on the Oxford to Fairford branch during the 1939-45 war. When laid in 1972, our main line was 520 yards (475.5 metres) long and ran to the end of the area occupied by the Society at that time. Towards the end of the 1970s, the Society had the opportunity to enlarge the Centre to its present 16 acre size, and in 1986, work started to lengthen the running line by a further 340 yards (311 metres). This now gives visitors a return journey of almost a mile (1.6 km). The new section was formally opened on 29th March 1987 and a plaque commemorates the grant from the English Tourist Board which helped to make all this possible.

A prominent feature of the route is the fixed distant signal warning drivers to slow their locomotives and be ready to stop at the end of the line. Distant signals may be passed at caution and act as the yellow aspect of a modern signal. They had distinctive fish tail notches cut in end of the arm to distinguish them from stop signals which must not be passed at danger (red aspect of a modern signal).

Along the new section of the line towards the Oxford end is an area which has been planted with trees. Like many similar areas alongside our country's railways, it has remained undisturbed and attracts unusual flora and fauna. This and other areas within the Centre have been fenced off to protect the natural beauty, and we would respectfully ask our

A view from inside the Transfer Shed of a train awaiting the 'right way'; the station is named Burlescombe which is where much of the broad gauge railway was discovered.

visitors not to cross the wire boundaries protecting these areas.

At the Oxford end of the line, work has commenced on building another station, but it will probably be many years before this is complete. The stone station buildings from Heyford on the Oxford to Birmingham main line have been painstakingly dismantled, numbered and stored for eventual re-erection on the platform. This will then enable passengers to alight at this end of the Centre, cross over to the Transfer Shed and take the branch line back to Didcot Halt.

THE TRAVELLING POST OFFICE (TPO)

When the railway network started taking shape in the 1830s and 1840s, the Post Office quickly perceived that sending letters by rail was infinitely quicker than the old horse drawn mail coaches. In 1838, the first Travelling Post Office was introduced in which letters were sorted en route, quickly followed by the mail exchange apparatus which allowed mail to be picked up and dropped at specific points without stopping the train.

With the introduction of modern diesel and electric

The Travelling Post Office in action with the mailbags about to be exchanged.

traction, train speeds and acceleration capabilities significantly increased, which brought about the demise of the mail exchange apparatus. The example at Didcot came from Penrith on the West Coast main line and is situated on the main demonstration line near the link line gate.

The TPO van No 814 is used to give demonstrations on dates advertised in our programme. No. 814 was built by the GWR in 1940 to replace an identical vehicle which had been destroyed in an accident. It regularly worked on the Paddington - Penzance TPO until 1959 when it was transferred to the South Eastern TPO train. The van is fitted with traducter arms on which mail bags are hung and swung out, allowing them to be deposited in the lineside nets. Simultaneously, mail bags are hung on the lineside apparatus and scooped up in the nets lowered from the side of the van. Since this operation took place at speeds of up to 80 mph on the main line, protection of both staff and mail was important. Beside the lineside apparatus you will see a small hut which was provided for the protection of the postmen operating the system. To protect the mail bags, they are enclosed in special leather pouches for both dropping and picking up.

RELICS DISPLAY

The small relics museum houses the smaller and perhaps less robust artefacts of the GWR Company history and the variety of materials is perhaps the most astonishing aspect of the display. Indeed, so numerous are these items that they far outnumber the locomotives and rolling stock. On display are such diverse items as clocks, uniforms, tickets, posters, books and publicity material, cutlery and silverware, toys, name and number plates cast iron ware, furniture, lamps and signalling equipment, and many, many more. A typical office of the 1930s has been constructed complete with clerk, furniture and stationery of the period.

The GWR had a vast army of staff to run its railway undertaking and their basic purpose in life was to shift passengers and freight quickly, efficiently and safely. Examples of the essential objects and administrative paperwork these people used in their daily routines are all on display. The aim of the museum is to gather a comprehensive record of all facets of the Company and its subsequent operations. Displays are located on the museum walls and in central display

A small selection of the material from the Great Western Railway hotels in the Relics Display.

cabinets and each one is "thematic" relating to a part of the business eg: Dinnerware, First Aid, Railway Police, etc. with the emphasis upon the quality of the items and the social history of the staff who used them.

The collection is administered by the Great Western Trust (Registered Charity 289008) whose Trustees are appointed by the Council of the Great Western Society. The Trust is a full member of the Area Museum Service for South East England.

Whilst the Museum does house a vast collection of books and paperwork, limitations on staff and accommodation unfortunately render impossible "public library" type access. Specific queries should be sent to the Curator but it must be remembered that the voluntary nature of his work severely limits time to answer such correspondence and patience is requested.

A large proportion of the material on display has been kindly donated by members and the general public since the Society was formed in 1961. We believe visitors will agree that their heirlooms could have no better home than the Museum, particularly for the enjoyment and education of future generations. The Trust welcomes any donations or loans of materials, subject of course to condition and duplication of items already held. Please speak to the Museum Stewards or write to the Curator, Didcot Railway Centre.

Visitors will no doubt be amazed at the volume of

Part of the office scene that has been created within the Relics Display.

artefacts on display. A vast collection of items are also held in reserve, not only for reasons of limited space, but also to ensure the variety of displays which are changed annually. Hence the Great Western Trust is looking forward to the fulfilment of future plans in which a much larger museum building is provided at Didcot. This will enable bigger and better displays with perhaps a model railway, audio/visual displays, and larger items such as horse drays and road vehicles.

A Reference Library Fund has been set up, details of which can be obtained from either the Museum or writing to the Curator.

DIDCOT VISITOR COMPLEX

When Didcot was an operational steam depot, it was provided with accommodation and services necessary for the well being of the staff employed there. These facilities were very primitive by modern day standards and were certainly not designed for the general public who were strictly prohibited from entering the site.

However, to fit its new role as a Railway Centre, appropriate public amenities have been added and enlarged to cater for the increasing number of visitors. The refreshment room was first opened in 1973 and this has subsequently been enlarged and incorporated into a larger complex with a visitor section and a smaller section for the volunteer workforce.

This visitor complex is located on the left of the Centre opposite the engine shed. The left hand wing provides a walk around shop and the right hand wing houses the Relics display with the refreshment room located in between. All three sections are fronted by a paved area and eventually this will be partly covered by a restored station canopy.

Toilet facilities are provided for ladies, located behind the shop area with access between the shop and information centre. Disabled and gentlemen's toilets are to be found near the cycle shed to the left of the visitor complex

The Information Centre and First Aid Post is just to the left of the visitor complex. If your require any information about the Centre, the Great Western Society, membership, forthcoming events, etc., please ask here or at the office in the engine shed when the Information Centre is not open - we will do our best to help you.

Finally, we have provided a picnic area just beyond the turntable where you can relax and watch the steam trains operating on both the main demonstration line and the branch line.

NAMES, NUMBERS AND CLASSES

The Great Western's broad gauge locomotives were identified only by names but when standard gauge locomotives were introduced they carried numbers whilst names were usually limited to the more prestigious locomotives.

Similar locomotives were grouped into classes and in later years these were identified by a class number which was the running number of the first built locomotive in the class. For example No. 6106 was a member of the 6100 class. Named locomotives such as No. 7808 Cookham Manor of the 7800 class were also known by the naming series – in this case "Manors".

The second digit of the class number usually carried through when there were more than 100 locomotives in the class, thus No. 6697 is a member of the 5600 class which used the fleet numbers 5600–5699 and 6600–6699. The large 5700 class ran out of X700 number series and later engines were numbered in the 3600, 4600 and 9600 series.

LOCOMOTIVES

The schoolboys standing on a footbridge overlooking an engine shed may have had no doubts of their ability to preserve a typical Great Western small locomotive and coach but none could have dreamed that in a short while their idea would blossom into a Society with a complete engine shed housing a comprehensive collection of Great Western locomotives as well as coaches and even goods wagons.

That the Great Western Railway developed uninterrupted for over a century means that many of the locomotives displayed today are part of a series that can be traced from Victorian times until the end of everyday steam traction in the mid 1960s. Main line express passenger locomotives, for instance, demonstrate a direct line of progression for nearly half a century until railway nationalisation in 1948.

By the late nineteenth century the Great Western had many standard locomotive types and when these needed renewal in the 1920s and 1930s updated versions were built. This gave a common theme throughout the fleet and many features were common to differing classes - although it is equally true to say that even within classes there were many detail differences, such as chimney styles. The continuity of Great Western locomotive design also means that exciting projects to reproduce earlier types of locomotive can be considered.

The initial locomotives in the Great Western Society's care came straight from service with British Railways - indeed it is

The first of the Castle class locomotives, No. 4073 Caerphilly Castle is on loan from the Science Museum. It has a small tender with 3,500 gallons water capacity as originally built and carries the paintwork from its overhaul at Swindon Works in 1961; to protect this it will normally be kept inside the Locomotive Works.

JOIN THE
GREAT WESTERN SOCIETY

The Great Western Society was started over 35 years ago by a group of schoolboys to preserve the spirit and style of the Great Western Railway at a time when the dieselisation and modernisation of British Railways were sweeping away the steam engines, signalling and stations of the traditional railway. The scenes you can see at Didcot Railway Centre were commonplace but without the foresight of the Society's founding members they would have gone forever.

Since its inception in 1961, the Great Western Society has assembled a more representative collection of locomotives, rolling stock and other artefacts of the Great Western Railway than exists of any other major railway company. Many items have been restored to operating condition but some still need considerable work and money expended to put them into working order and keep them running.

Our achievements are the results of volunteer effort by our membership, by becoming a member you can help in a practical way by coming along to Didcot and taking an active part in locomotive or carriage restoration, track laying or other engineering activities. Skilled or unskilled you will be welcome. You could also take part in our Steamday activities with the aim of becoming a Station Master or ultimately an engine driver.

In addition to our activities at Didcot we have groups in Bristol, the East Midlands, London, the North West, Oxford, South Wales, the South West, Swindon and Taunton, which organise meetings and other activities in their areas and some are engaged in specific projects at Didcot. Regular newsletters keep member fully informed about Society events and the illustrated magazine 'Great Western Echo' supplements Society news with features on the GWR. Except on a few special occasions members enjoy free admission to Didcot events and receive priority in booking on any Society steam railtours on the main line.

We are an independent organisation relying on income from the subscriptions of over 5,000 members and events at Didcot. Whether or not you can play an active part in its activities you will be welcomed as a member of the Great Western Society.

Great Western Society
Application for membership

Subscription rates (please tick appropriate box)

- ❑ Full £18
- ❑ Junior £10
- ❑ Over 60 £10
- ❑ Family £24 (husband, wife & children under 18)
- ❑ Over 60 (husband & wife) £12
- ❑ Life £300
- ❑ Life husband & wife £400
- ❑ Life over 60 £150
- ❑ Life over 60 husband & wife £200

Annual subscriptions are renewed 12 months from date of joining. There is an enrolment fee of £2. All these rates include VAT.

I enclose remittance for	£	p
Enrolment fee	2	00
Subscription		
GWS members' badge (price £2)		
Didcot Railway Centre Guide (price £3)		
Donation		
Total Enclosed		

or debit my Visa/Mastercard

Number............... / .... / .... / ....

Expiry Date .... Signature ....

Name (Mr/Mrs/Miss)..

Full address..

....

.... Postcode ....

Date of Birth *(if under 18 years)* ....

Occupation ....

Date .... Signed..

Family membership: please list names of all persons to be included

Name	Date of birth *(if under 18)*
....	....
....	....
....	....
....	....
....	....
....	

In the case of an application from a person under 18 years of age (including family members) the following clause must be signed by the parent or guardian of the applicant before the application can be considered.

I ....

being the parent or guardian of..

...........................hereby certify that I shall be responsible for his/her observing and conforming with the Memorandum, Articles and Rules of the Company from time to time in force and direction given by responsible officers until he/she reaches the age of 18.

Signed .... *(parent/guardian)*

Cheques, etc should be crossed, made payable to Great Western Society Limited and forwarded with this form to Great Western Society Ltd., Didcot, Oxfordshire, OX11 7NJ.

For official use only: Membership No.

4/97

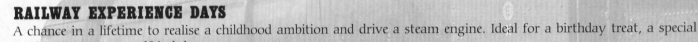

RAILWAY EXPERIENCE DAYS

A chance in a lifetime to realise a childhood ambition and drive a steam engine. Ideal for a birthday treat, a special anniversary or pure self-indulgence.

The Day includes a tour of the Centre including the workships and signalboxes with an experienced guide, driving and firing the locomotive and being guard of the train, and luncheon in the refreshment room.

CORPORATE ENTERTAINMENT

Didcot Railway Centre is a popular venue for events of many kinds including conferences, product launches, a location for filming or corporate hospitality. You can hire a steam train for a corporate Railway Experience Day.

The Centre is ideally situated with direct access by Inter-City train and near the M4 and M40 motorways.

a salutary thought that even some Great Western thoroughbreds have now been in preservation longer than they served the GWR and BR! If caring for and maintaining these veterans is an achievement for what are mainly small volunteer teams of Great Western Society members working in their spare time, then consider later additions to the collection which came from scrapyards where the ravages of weather, removal of ferrous fittings and other spare parts has required the complete rebuilding of such locomotives by the same small teams.

In condition terms, the fleet at Didcot can be put into three categories. The "runners" are those locomotives which are operational and available to work on Steamdays. Others are complete - and indeed have run in preservation - but now await or are undergoing further attention, sometimes to mechanical wear and tear but more usually to the boiler. The final category are those are which have not run since withdrawal from everyday service - that is for three decades or more - and these often incomplete locomotives are either undergoing or awaiting their turn for complete restoration.

The locomotives to be seen at Didcot can vary from time to time and those currently "on shed" - and their condition - can be ascertained by reference to the Running Board on the wall of the main shed near the office.

Operational locomotives are sometimes loaned for operation on steam railways or to other preservation centres while on occasions other locomotives visit Didcot. Some of these may work in on main line railtours and may be on the depot for just a few hours' servicing or stay for several weeks between main line workings. Currently the Centre is host to *No. 4073 Caerphilly Castle* which is on loan from the Science Museum.

The Great Western's main locomotive works was at Swindon and most GWR locomotives were built there although some, particularly freight tank locomotives, were built by contractors. As part of the railway grouping in 1923 many locomotives were absorbed from constituent railways. Over its last 25 years the GWR's locomotive fleet was around 3,900 strong.

Although the collection is largely Great Western in origin there are some non-GWR or later items. Visiting locomotives, particularly, are of varied origins while "modern" diesel shunters perform a valuable role in moving stock around the Centre - a local precedent for non-steam traction was set by the GWR as long ago as 1927 when a petrol engined shunter was used at its Didcot Provender Store.

The locomotives at Didcot can be be described within four headings - the large passenger engines, other tender engines, tank engines and others - non steam or non GWR.

LARGE PASSENGER ENGINES

From the early years of the century until the end of steam, the Great Western developed a series of 4-6-0 locomotives for main line express and, later, more secondary work. Representatives of most of the later types can be seen at Didcot and there are plans to reconstruct an earlier version. They are described here in descending order of power:

The Kings

The Kings are the most powerful 4-6-0 locomotives ever to have worked in this country. Built at Swindon between 1927 and 1930 they were used until 1962 on the Great Western's heaviest and most prestigious express trains. *No. 6023 King Edward II* was initially rescued from a South Wales scrapyard by Harvey's of Bristol and in 1990 it was transferred to Didcot where better facilities are available for its full restoration. After withdrawal from service the locomotive languished in a South Wales scrapyard for many years and during this time several of its driving wheels were damaged, necessitating the making of patterns and casting replacements. This locomotive will be restored to its original condition with

---

WHEEL ARRANGEMENTS

Apart from individual numbers and classes, locomotives are further identified by the number of wheels. This system uses the Whyte notation, listing in sequence the number of small carrying wheels at the front, the number of driving wheels, and then carrying wheels to the rear. So, most Great Western large passenger tender locomotives were 4-6-0 (four leading carrying wheels, six driving wheels but no rear carrying wheels) while 1466, the Society's first locomotive, is an 0-4-2T, the T denoting a tank engine with coal and water carried on the locomotive rather than in a separate tender.

a single chimney replacing the double chimney fitted by BR in the 1950s.

Sister engine *No. 6024 King Edward I*, which is to be seen at Didcot from time to time, retains its double chimney. King Edward I is owned by the 6024 Preservation Society and following its restoration this locomotive is often used on main line steam excursions. The chimney, safety valve cover and cab have been reduced in height to give it increased route availability over Railtrack's lines.

The Castles

The mainstay of Great Western express trains from the 1920s, the Castles were the most successful of the company's locomotive designs and the last batch, bringing the class total to 171, was completed by British Railways in 1950. Like the Kings they are four-cylinder engines - two inside and two

Top: No. 5051 Earl Bathurst (or Drysllwyn Castle).

Left: The majesty of the Kings: No. 6024 King Edward I.

Below: Inside the Lifting Shop: the boiler of No. 6023 King Edward II is reunited with its frames.

outside. The class was the first to have the large side-windowed cab which is characteristic of all the larger tender engines at Didcot.

No. 5051 Drysllwyn Castle was obtained from a scrapyard in 1970 and 10 years later after a full restoration was returned to service and made a number of successful main line runs. Its Welsh name is appropriate for a locomotive which spent all its working days based in the Principality but this name was not carried for long after the locomotive's completion in 1936 – a year later it was renamed *Earl Bathurst*. Both sets of nameplates are available at Didcot and they are exchanged from time-to-time.

A second Castle currently at Didcot is *No. 4073 Caerphilly Castle*, the first of the class to be completed, in 1923, and which was displayed at the British Empire Exhibition at Wembley the following year. From 1961 until the autumn of 1996 the locomotive was housed at the Science Museum. To allow room for new developments at the museum the locomotive will, for some years, be housed at Didcot where it will usually be on static display in the Locomotive Works. The expectation is that it will eventually be displayed in its birthplace of Swindon.

The Halls

The Hall class mixed traffic locomotives were the largest two cylinder engines among the later standard 4-6-0s. From 1928, 259 were built to Collett's original design and a further 71 Modified Halls were built in the 1940s under Hawksworth,

The Churchward 2-6-0 No. 5322.

the main distinguishing feature of the later locomotives being the extended frames which can be seen below the smokebox.

No. 5900 Hinderton Hall was built in 1931 and like many of its stablemates at Didcot has been restored to main line condition since being brought from a scrapyard.

Our Modified Hall is *No. 6998 Burton Agnes Hall* which worked the Western Region's last main line steam hauled train in January 1966 and was immediately acquired by the GWS – the Society's first express passenger engine. Actually built by British Railways in 1949 the locomotive has the last design of tender produced for the GWR, identified by its high flat sides.

The Hall class was derived from the Saint class dating from 1902, the major difference being the Hall's smaller diameter driving wheels. Didcot's third Hall *(No. 4942 Maindy Hall)* was rescued from a scrapyard in the 1970s with the long term aim of using it as the basis on which to recreate a Saint class locomotive. For many years other work took priority but, with the aim of completion in 2002, the project is now being progressed with the manufacture of new driving wheel and cylinder castings.

Smaller 4-6-0s

Apart from the post-war Counties, the last two standard 4-6-0 classes for the GWR were the Grange and Manor. The Granges were a smaller version of the Hall and none of the 80 built survived into preservation. The Manor was the smallest of the 4-6-0s and their lighter weight allowed their use on a

CHIEF MECHANICAL ENGINEERS	
In over a century the Great Western only had six Chief Mechanical Engineers (the term Locomotive Superintendent was used in the 19th century). They were:	
Sir Daniel Gooch	1837–1864
Joseph Armstrong	1864–1877
William Dean	1877–1902
George Jackson Churchward	1902–1921
Charles B. Collett	1921–1941
Frederick W. Hawksworth	1941–1947

Rolling stock from the later four CMEs is on display at Didcot, while the locomotive collection is representative of the Churchward, Collett and Hawksworth eras.

Heavy Freight 2-8-0 No. 3822 heads a mixed rake of wagons on the main demonstration line.

wider range of secondary main lines and cross country routes. *No. 7808 Cookham Manor* was built in 1938 and was another locomotive to be purchased for preservation direct from British Railways.

OTHER TENDER LOCOMOTIVES

The Granges and Manors were to some extent built to replace smaller locomotives and No. 5322 is representative of these earlier classic Churchward 2-6-0s. This is the only tender locomotive at Didcot with the older cab design without side windows (later additions to the class had that feature) and when built it had inside steam pipes between the cylinders and smokebox, although outside pipes were added later. Built at Swindon in 1917, No. 5322 was immediately shipped out to France where, working for the Railway Operating Department of the Army, she hauled supply trains from the Channel ports to the battle lines. The locomotive returned to the GWR in 1919 and between 1928 and 1944 was altered to a 8300 class, with modifications to reduce wheel flange wear on curvaceous track in the West of England.

To haul heavy freight and coal trains the GWR introduced a class of large 2-8-0 locomotives in 1903. No. 3822 is a later version (for instance with the side windowed cab and with outside steam pipes) built in 1940. Although it was one of the last Didcot locomotives to be rescued from a scrapyard, restoration was commenced quickly and it appears in the wartime black livery it carried when new.

The original GWR lines were built to broad gauge (7ft) and although this was abolished in 1892 a section of broad gauge railway has been relaid within the Centre. To operate on this a reproduction broad gauge locomotive is being constructed in Didcot Locomotive Works by the Firefly Project. The Firefly class of 2-2-2 tender locomotives was, in 1839, the first locomotive type designed by Sir Daniel Gooch for the Great Western Railway.

TANK LOCOMOTIVES

The GWR had a large fleet of tank engines ranging from small four-wheeled shunters to 2-8-2 locomotives for hauling heavy freight trains, and almost as large a variety of passenger tank locomotives.

Numerically the largest type of tank loco was the 0-6-0 with Pannier Tanks, characteristic of, though not unique to, the GWR. While larger tank engines usually had side tanks resting on the footplate alongside the boiler, many smaller tank locomotives had saddle tanks over the boiler which had the advantage of allowing access to valve gear between the locomotive's frames. However as engines became larger the saddle tanks reduced the driver's visibility, a drawback overcome by the use of pannier tanks along the side of the boiler. In addition to the many hundreds built with pannier tanks, many early GWR saddle tank locomotives were later rebuilt with pannier tanks.

Many of the GWR's smaller tank locomotives were absorbed from small railways in South Wales as part of the railway grouping in 1923. Typical of these 0-4-0 saddle tank shunting locomotives are No. 1338, built by Kitson of Leeds for the Cardiff Railway in 1898 and which was not withdrawn from BR service until 1963, and No. 1340, built by the Avonside Engine Company for the Alexandra Dock & Railway Co in Newport. Entering GWR stock in 1923 it was sold for industrial use (initially at a colliery and later at a paper mill) in 1934 and was bought for preservation in 1968.

No. 1363, constructed in 1910, is a somewhat larger six-wheeled saddle tank and differs from the previous two in that it was built by and for the Great Western. Although it is the only remaining example of a Swindon-built saddle tank it is not a typical example as it has outside cylinders and a short wheelbase, for shunting in yards and docks where there were sharp curves. The design largely followed that of similar engines absorbed from the Cornwall Minerals Railway. When first purchased for preservation it was kept for several years at the Society's then depot at Bodmin.

No. 1466 was the first locomotive to be preserved by the Great Western Society and is an 0-4-2T of the type usually used in conjunction with a single auto carriage. The train could be driven from the engine or by means of a system of rodding from rudimentary controls in a cab at the further end of the coach, thus simplifying operations on busy suburban or branch lines. Built in the 1930s these locomotives were originally numbered in the 4800 series.

The 863 locomotives of the 5700 class of 0-6-0PT were the Great Western's most prolific class. Two locomotives represent the class at Didcot, No. 3650 was purchased after use by Stephenson Clarke Contractors in South Wales while No. 3738 spent some years in a scrapyard before being rescued for restoration. While largely used on shunting and short distance freight duties, 5700 class locomotives also worked local passenger trains.

For suburban and middle distance passenger work the Great Western used many 2-6-2T (Prairie) locomotives which are usually referred to as small or large - reflecting wheel diameter and overall size. No. 5572 is typical of the smaller variety and was built in 1929. In 1952 it was equipped for auto-train operation (see No. 1466) in South Wales. It was saved from the scrapyard by the GWS Taunton Group in the

mid 1970s and initial restoration was started at their Taunton site before the locomotive was moved to Didcot in 1977 and restoration completed .

The largest of the "Prairies" was the 6100 class which worked suburban services from Paddington to the Thames Valley. No. 6106 was bought out of service by a GWS member and after an initial stay at the Society's first HQ in a goods shed at Taplow was the first GWS locomotive to move to Didcot in November 1967. No. 4144, a similar but less

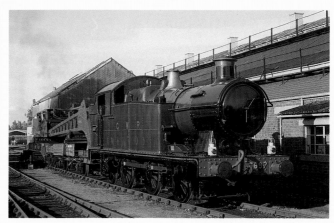
0-6-2 tank No. 6697 with the 50 ton steam crane.

Getting up steam for an operating day, No. 1466 (left) and No. 5572 outside the engine shed.

'Large Prairie' tank engine No. 6106.

23

powerful engine, was among a number of locomotives acquired from a scrapyard in 1970 and is in the throes of restoration.

Many of the pre-grouping railways working in the South Wales Valleys used 0-6-2T locomotives for coal traffic and in 1924 the Great Western introduced their standard version, the 5600 class. In all 200 were built, the last 50 by Armstrong Whitworth of Newcastle in 1928 and No. 6697 was one of these. All passed into British Railways stock and No. 6697 was the last to be withdrawn, in 1966, going straight into preservation.

The largest tank engines built by the Great Western are represented by No. 7202. Weighing 93 tons in working order these were the GWR's longest and heaviest locomotives. They were rebuilt from 2-8-0T locos (No. 7202 was originally 2-8-0T No. 5277) used for hauling coal trains in South Wales but which had limited coal capacity for working longer distances - the enlarged 7200 class were able to work coal trains right through to the West of England or London.

RAILCAR, OTHER LOCOMOTIVES and CRANES AT DIDCOT

The Great Western experimented with its first petrol-electric railcar in 1911 but it is best known for the series of diesel railcars built by AEC of Southall and which entered service from 1933. Powered by two 9.6 litre diesel engines the drive was mechanical. As well as passenger accommodation the cars included a small luggage and guard's van and a driving compartment at each end. The first of these streamlined cars included a small buffet and were used on high speed long

Diesel railcar No. 22 alongside its modern counterpart, a Thames Turbo used on the local trains through Didcot.

distance services but their popularity outgrew the passenger capacity so, like later cars, they were moved onto more local services. Diesel railcar **No. 22** dates from 1940 and has the later, more angular, Swindon built body on its AEC chassis. These later cars had conventional drawgear and could haul an auto trailer or horse box. The last GWR railcars built were in 2-car sets, truly the forerunner of the diesel multiple unit trains of today.

Apart from the Great Western stock at Didcot there is a number of other steam locomotives normally based here.

No. 1 Bonnie Prince Charlie is not dissimilar to the 0-4-0ST locomotives which originated from the South Wales railways. However, this one was built in 1949 (by Robert Stephenson & Hawthorns) and worked at coal wharfs at Poole and Southampton before being acquired by the Salisbury

Steam Locomotive Preservation Trust. Its main GWR connection must now be that it is one of the longest resident of Didcot's locomotives and has spent longer here than it did in commercial service!

No. 2 Pontyberem was built for the Burry Port & Gwendreath Valley Railway by Avonside in 1900. Had it not already been sold out of service - to a colliery company - it would have become a Great Western engine when the BP&GV was absorbed into the GWR in 1923. However, but for its sale it may not have survived long enough to be rescued for preservation. Awaiting its turn for restoration, when completed it will make an interesting comparison with No. 1363, the GWR 0-6-0ST of the same era.

No. 5 Shannon should perhaps be listed as a Great Western locomotive as the GWR bought it for preservation as long ago

Two visiting engines 'on shed' at Didcot: British Railways standard design 2-6-4 tank No. 80079 from the Severn Valley Railway and Southern Railway Merchant Navy class No. 35005 Canadian Pacific.

British Railways 350hp diesel shunting locomotive No. 08 604 bearing a ficticious War Department livery.

No. 1338 is a small 0-4-0 saddle tank built originally for the Cardiff Railway.

as 1945! The locomotive is the oldest at Didcot, having been built in 1857 for the Sandy & Potton Railway in Bedfordshire. Subsequently this line was taken over by the London & North Western Railway and Shannon was used as a shunter at Crewe before being sold in 1878 to the Wantage Tramway which ran a roadside line linking that town with Wantage Road GWR station. On the Wantage Tramway the locomotive was numbered 5 and known as Jane. When the tramway closed in 1945 the GWR arranged for No. 5 to be displayed at Wantage Road station and subsequently the locomotive came

into the care of the National Railway Museum who put it on loan to Didcot, just a few miles from Wantage. Although a tank engine, the tanks are not obvious as they are Well Tanks housed between the frames of the locomotive.

There are also two steam cranes at Didcot. British Railways retained some steam cranes long after steam locomotives had been withdrawn and **RS1054** is a 50 ton breakdown crane built in 1930 by Cowan and Sheldon for the London Midland & Scottish Railway and only withdrawn from Edinburgh Haymarket depot in 1987. A much smaller

The oldest locomotive at Didcot, Wantage Tramway No. 5 Shannon.

A regular visitor and a firm favourite with children, Thomas is the main character in the late Rev. W. Awdry's railway series of books.

(5 ton capacity) steam crane came from industrial use as did a diesel crane of similar capacity.

The Great Western had used some small internal combustion locomotives for mainly internal use from the 1920s and in the next decade tried a larger diesel-electric shunter. Similar diesel-electrics became the standard BR shunting loco and some are still in use today - known as class 08. In 1994 the GWS acquired **08 604** (previously D 3771) for shunting purposes at Didcot when no steam locomotive is available. With its 350hp engine, it is more powerful than **DL 26** a former National Coal Board Hunslet built 264hp diesel-mechanical shunter which has been at Didcot since 1978.

COACHES

If the Great Western was renowned for a highly standardised locomotive fleet then its coaching fleet was much the opposite. However, the collection at Didcot allows the progress made over the years to be followed.

At the end of its independent existence the GWR had just under 6,000 passenger carrying vehicles. The range was enormous from humble third class non-corridor compartment coaches to the plush Ocean Liner Saloons. Slip coaches, Sleeping Cars and Restaurant Cars bore the same chocolate and cream livery as single coaches used on rural push-pull trains and vintage stock eeking out its last days on

SAINT PROJECT

When locomotive No. 2999 Lady of Legend steams at Didcot for the first time in 2002 it will be more than another locomotive restoration. Nor even just a recreation of an Edwardian locomotive. It will celebrate the centenary of Great Western Railway express passenger 4-6-0 locomotives and will also mark the foresight of those Great Western Society members who first mooted the project over thirty years previously.

In the early years of the 20th century, Churchward had conceived a standard series of express locomotives and the first to be built, in 1902, was No. 100 - later No. 2900 William Dean. This was a two-cylinder locomotive and a quarter of a century later was the basis of the Hall class and subsequently other two-cylinder 4-6-0 locomotives. Contemporary with No. 100 was a more powerful four cylinder 4-6-0 No. 40 (later No. 4000) North Star, the initial engine of the Star class from which the Castles and Kings evolved.

Of the 92 Saints built (as ever, there were variations among this total) over half survived into British Railways ownership but the last were withdrawn in 1953 - eight years before the formation of the Great Western Society. However, with the Saint class the basis of the later Halls the Society developed the idea of using an unrestored Hall to recreate a Saint. So in the early 1970s No. 4942 Maindy Hall was rescued from a scrapyard and moved for storage at Didcot with this long-term aim.

In the mid 1990s, the dream began to take shape with the launch of the Saint Project Appeal to enable completion of the task by 2002, the centenary of the first Saint. Using the boiler and basic frames of No. 4942, it is intended to recreate the original Saint design with inside steam pipes, straight frames and square drop ends, and lever reversing. In their early years some Saints were modified to 4-4-2 (Atlantic) wheel arrangement for comparative tests and it is intended that an "Atlantic Option" will enable the recreated locomotive to be converted to this configuration from time-to-time.

The major difference from a Hall class locomotive is the size of the wheels. For the driving wheels, a pattern was made and six new wheels cast, also needed are new tyres and axles... it is not inappropriate to point out that that simple sentence covers several months work and expense! The bogie wheels came from an unlikely source - originally from a Castle class locomotive, for the past thirty or more years they have carried a radio telescope at Jodrell Bank. Like the new driving wheels, these need new tyres and axles. Other castings under way include injectors and the largest single new item, the inside steam pipe cylinder block.

When the locomotive emerges from Didcot Locomotive Works in 2002 it will be resplendent in the handsome fully-lined Edwardian GWR livery and will carry No. 2999 (in sequence from the numerical last Saint), while a magazine competition led to the name "Lady of Legend" being chosen.

Clerestory roofed third class compartment coach No. 1941.

secondary services. As well as passenger-carrying vehicles, another 2,500 vehicles - known as Brown vehicles from their colour scheme - could run in passenger trains for traffic such as parcels, horses and milk. No less than 8,000 vehicles serviced the railway itself and while many of these were humble ballast wagons a number were former coaches and their continued use in this background role meant the survival of early stock which would not have otherwise been around when the railway preservation movement started.

The collection of Great Western coaches at Didcot is probably the most comprehensive in existence of any of the prenationalised railways. With their largely wooden body construction - metal panelling was introduced in the 1900s but wooden framing was used throughout the GWR's existence – coaches are much more vulnerable to the ravages of time and weather than locomotives and often need complete rebuilding to restore their former glory.

Over 40 vehicles cover the period from the 1887s to the 1950s with **6824** the oldest, dating from April 1887. Originally built to run on the broad gauge and subsequently converted to standard gauge, it avoided destruction by spending many years as a chicken shed after withdrawal from railway service. Restoration is a major undertaking but it is planned to convert **6824** back to its original broad gauge condition.

Other vehicles dating from the late l9th century (**290**, **416** and **975**) are among those which survived for preservation because they spent many years as service

vehicles. These four- or six-wheel coaches were very basic having a low roof with no clerestory and sparse upholstery. Rather better appointed is **2511**, a third class family saloon which could be booked by families or groups and attached to scheduled trains. Restoration of 2511 - which spent many years as a riverside cottage and happily retained much of the original furniture and fittings - is well advanced.

Coach bogies were first used in the 1870s and by the early 20th century even coaches for less important trains were being built with bogies, albeit that the Great Western used an unusual design with no centre pivot, being fixed to the underframe by scroll irons, which while giving a smooth ride was expensive to build and maintain. Didcot's early bogie coaches (**1357** and **1941**) also demonstrate the return to clerestory roofs which gave additional space for ventilation and lighting. Gas lighting with elaborate fittings, which can be seen in 1941, replaced oil as the light source. Of similar age is a Dining Car (**9520**) body which is mounted on a later chassis. This is the earliest example of a gangwayed (that is with connections to the adjoining coaches) coach at Didcot.

The next type of carriage brought designs well into the 20th century. Gone was the clerestory, replaced by a high elliptical roof, while the windows previously in the clerestory moved above the main side windows giving this distinctive stock the name Toplights - applied to both main line stock with corridor connections and coaches built for suburban traffic (see 3755 and 3756). Electric lighting became standard

Centenary dining car No. 9635 on the traverser outside the carriage shed.

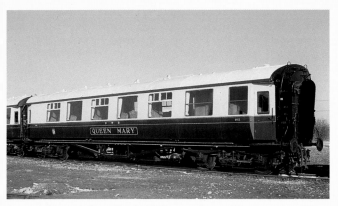

Super Saloon carriage No. 9112 Queen Mary

with dynamos and battery boxes replacing gas cylinders on the underframes and the Toplights also introduced conventional centre pivoted bogies.

With a length of 70ft (21.35m) and built to the width limit of the loading gauge, early Toplights (**3299**) were nicknamed Dreadnoughts after the battleship of the time. The 70ft length was used from time to time but the more usual coach length was just under 60ft (18.3m). Later Toplights (**7538**) were to the shorter length and introduced steel external panels instead of wood .

By 1923, the toplights were replaced by larger side windows (**7976**). To reduce the length of flexible gangway needed between carriages bow ended coaches (**4553, 5085**) were introduced another trademark of these vehicles being the 7ft (2.13m) wheelbase bogie.

Collett's standard coaches of the 1930s reverted to 9ft (2.74m) bogies and flat ends (**5787, 5952**). Despite the introduction of side corridors many years previously these were the first coaches to have large windows on the corridor side. The interior design was, however, little changed from coaches produced in the early part of the century.

By 1937 coaches built for excursion traffic (**1289**) had an open plan interior without compartments. The interior was pleasantly styled in the typical square decor of the time in polished woods. Even in corridor stock, compartments still had individual exterior doors but 1939 saw a complete change (**536, 1111**) with each compartment having a large window and access only from the corridor. Internally the polished

wood of earlier years was replaced by cream panelling. Further examples (**7285, 7313, 7371**) were completed during the war.

Perhaps the most luxurious coaches ever designed for use by fare paying passengers were introduced in 1931. Known as the Super Saloons, only eight were built (no less than three **9112, 9113** and **9118** - are at Didcot) and all carried the names of members of the Royal family. They were built specifically for use in boat trains connecting with the transatlantic liners calling at Plymouth.

Two new trains were built specially for the Cornish Riviera Express in 1935 - the Great Western's Centenary Year. Only one vehicle (Dining Car **9635**) survives of this Centenary Stock and it is at Didcot along with Special Saloon **9002** which was used for high ranking railway and government officials.

Perhaps the biggest gap in the collection is a later suburban traffic coach, the two examples at Didcot (**3755** and **3756**) being Toplight style 1921-built City stock, so-called because they were used in through trains continuing over the Metropolitan Railway from Paddington to the City. They are good examples of suburban coaches seating five a side in narrow compartments and the pair survived after use as miners' transport at Glyn Corrwg in South Wales. Coach **3755** has been restored and carries the chocolate lake livery used by the GWR between 1908 and 1922.

Corridor composite (first and third classes) No. 7313 in the austerity reddish brown livery adopted during the second world war.

Unusually for the period, most of the auto-trailers had open saloons; this is No. 190 as restored in 1995 complete with hanging straps for standing passengers.

The original aim of the Great Western Society was the preservation of a typical Great Western auto-train. To accompany locomotive No. 1466, coach 231 was purchased - the first coach for the GWS. While this appears to be a typical GWR autocoach it was in fact one of a batch built by BR in the early 1950s. Subsequently three GWR built autocoaches have been acquired (92, 190 and 212). Many GWR autocoaches were rebuilt from self-propelled steam railmotors and 212 is an example. As it has still to be restored, consideration is being given to rebuilding 212 as a steam railmotor again.

The last Great Western coach designs (7372) came from Hawksworth and were introduced after the war. Externally identified by their bow ends, almost flat sides and shaped ends to the roof, the interiors followed the same general layout as the last pre-war coaches. Panelled veneers were fitted to line the compartment walls to just below the ceiling while later versions (2202) were built into BR days in 1950 and featured a brighter interior with panels lined with an enamelled hardboard. Among the last GWR design coaches to be built a batch of Hawksworth Sleeping Cars (9083).

In addition to these passenger coaches, the GWS collection includes a number of other vehicles which could be included in passenger trains and were categorised as passenger stock. Those at Didcot include full brake vans (111, 933, 1159, 1184) used for carrying luggage, parcels, mails and newspapers, a Siphon G (2726) for carrying milk churns,

carriage trucks - for carrying horse drawn and later motor road vehicles - (484, 565), and a Travelling Post Office vehicle (814) which is sometimes demonstrated at Didcot using the lineside mailbag pick up and set down apparatus.

There are also some vehicles designed by British Railways: a standard Mark I vehicle is used as a support coach on main line steam runs and examples of BR Mk I coaches and a Mk III sleeping car are used for accommodation for volunteers working at Didcot.

GOODS WAGONS

In 1934 the author of the GWR publication "Cheltenham Flyer - a Railway Book for Boys of All Ages" could write of railway freight services: "we depend upon them for our very existence. I wonder if you realise that nearly all your food, clothing, fuel, letters and papers, practically everything you eat, wear or use comes to you by railway." At that time freight receipts outweighed those from passenger traffic and the Great Western owned some 90,000 merchandise wagons of various types to which some thousands of privately-owned wagons based on the system must be added.

So the 40 or so goods wagons in the GWS collection show some of the variety of vehicles which were needed to carry both the commonplace and the unusual. For the specialist railway historian they demonstrate the development of various forms of braking, construction and such like which developed over the years.

No. 105860 is an insulated van for the carriage of meat, codenamed Mica B.

The simplest wagons were open trucks for carrying coal and other minerals. A considerable amount of general merchandise also travelled in such wagons, often sheeted over with a tarpaulin to give protection from the weather. More perishable traffic was moved in covered vans - including some iron bodied ones though most were of wood - and these basic types formed the majority of the fleet and are well represented at Didcot.

Specialist vehicles among the GWS collection include tanks for oil products and similar vehicles for milk traffic - which was carried in individual churns until the 1930s; refrigerated vans for carrying meat or fish and heated vans for carrying bananas; and vans adapted for carrying grain or tea. For heavier loads there are the flat wagons - often bogied - for carrying heavy machinery or girders, and there is even a wagon for carrying plate glass in crates.

There are also vehicles used for the railway's own purposes by signalling, track and breakdown crews, and to complete the train the brake van - of which there are three (dating from 1899 to 1950) at Didcot.

While most are preserved for their historical interest - the majority are over 70 years old - some, such as ballast or coal wagons or the well trolleys used to support locomotive boilers during restoration work, still play a useful role both within and sometimes beyond Didcot Railway Centre.

Most GWR wagons display code names which were used to describe their uses and to readily identify them to railway staff or when used in telegraphed messages. Some are relatively obvious such as Bloater to describe a fish van but others such as Mink (a covered van for general use) are purely convenient codes. Some, such as Toad for Brake Vans, were in general railway use.

The auto-train in action with the driver in the cab of trailer No. 190, with locomotive No. 1466 and trailer No. 231.

LOCOMOTIVE AND ROLLING STOCK LIST

This list covers all Locomotives and Rolling Stock preserved under the auspices of the Great Western Society Ltd. as at 1st April, 1997. The stock is based at the Society's Didcot Railway Centre and may usually be seen there. Sometimes loans - usually of locomotives - are made to other preserved railways or centres and on occasion visiting stock may be seen at Didcot.

While much of the stock is fully restored and readily identifiable, there are other items which are stored, sometimes in pieces, awaiting restoration and it may prove a challenge to recognise these!

The list is in numerical order for locomotives and other motive power, coaching stock, goods wagons and miscellaneous stock. The number used is that with which the vehicle has been restored; unrestored items usually carry their 'as acquired' identity, for instance some carriages and wagons were converted for special or utility uses later in their lives and renumbered -they will retain these identities until restored.

GREAT WESTERN STEAM LOCOMOTIVES

Number	Name	Class	Built by	Year Built	Wheel Arrangement	Withdrawn (by GWR/BR)	Into GWS Collection	First used in Preservation
1338		CR	Kitson & Co., Leeds No. 3799	1898	0-4-0ST	1963	1987	-
1340	TROJAN	ADR	Avonside Engine Co., Bristol No. 1386	1897	0-4-0ST	1932IN	1968	-
1363		1361	GWR Swindon	1910	0-6-0ST	1962	1964	1964
1466	(originally numbered 4866)	4800	GWR Swindon	1936	0-4-2T	1963	1964	1964
3650		5700	GWR Swindon	1939	0-6-0PT	1963SC	1969	-
3738		5700	GWR Swindon	1937	0-6-0PT	1965	1974	1977
3822		2884	GWR Swindon	1940	2-8-0	1964	1976	1985
4073	CAERPHILLY CASTLE	4073	GWR Swindon	1923	4-6-0	1960	1996SM	-
4144		5101	GWR Swindon	1946	2-6-2T	1965	1974	
4942	MAINDY HALL	4900	GWR Swindon	1929	4-6-0	1963	1974	LL
5051	DRYSLLWYN CASTLE/ EARL BATHURST	4073	GWR Swindon	1936	4-6-0	1963	1970	1980
5322		4300	GWR Swindon	1917	2-6-0	1964	1969	1971
5572		4575	GWR Swindon	1929	2-6-2T	1962	1971	1985
5900	HINDERTON HALL	4900	GWR Swindon	1931	4-6-0	1963	1971	1976
6023	KING EDWARD I	6000	GWR Swindon	1930	4-6-0	1962	1990	
6024	KING EDWARD II	6000	GWR Swindon	1930	4-6-0	1962	1990KE	1989
6106		6100	GWR Swindon	1931	2-6-2T	1965	1966	1966
6697		5600	Armstrong Whitworth, Newcastle No. 985	1928	0-6-2T	1966	1966	1967
6998	BURTON AGNES HALL	6959	BR Swindon	1949	4-6-0	1966	1966	1966
7202		7200	GWR Swindon - rebuilt from No. 5277	1934	2-8-2T	1964	1974	-
7808	COOKHAM MANOR	7800	GWR Swindon	1938	4-6-0	1966	1966	1966

OTHER STEAM LOCOMOTIVES

Number	Name	Class	Built by	Year Built	Wheel Arrangement	Withdrawn (by GWR/BR)	Into GWS Collection	First used in Preservation
1	BONNIE PRINCE CHARLIE	-	Robert Stephenson & Hawthorns No. 7544	1949	0-4-0ST	CW	1969	1969
2	PONTYBEREM	BPGV	Avonside Engine Co., Bristol No. 1421	1900	0-6-0ST	MA	1970	-
5	SHANNON/JANE	SPR	George England & Co., London	1857	0-4-0WT	WT	1969NR	1969
	FIRE FLY	BG	Firefly Project, Didcot	u/c	2-2-2	–	1988	-

DIESEL RAILCAR AND LOCOMOTIVES

Number	Name	Class	Built by	Year Built	Wheel Arrangement	Withdrawn (by GWR/BR)	Into GWS Collection	First used in Preservation
22	(Passenger Railcar)	Dia A1 Lot 1635	Associated Equipment Co., Southall (chassis)/GWR Swindon (body)	1940	4w-4w	1962	1967	1968
DL26		-	Hunslet Engine Co., Leeds No. 5238	1957	0-6-0DM	NC	1978	1978
08 604	(originally No. D 3771)	08	BR, Derby	1959	0-6-0DE	1994	1994PO	1995

NOTES

Class

CR – Built for Cardiff Railway (No.5). Absorbed into GWR stock 1923.

ADR – Built for Alexandra (Newport & South Wales) Docks and Railway (named TROJAN but un-numbered). Absorbed into GWR stock 1923.

BPGV – Built for Burry Port & Gwendraeth Valley Railway. Sold for industrial use 1914.

SPR – Built for Sandy & Potton Railway. Later to London & North Western Railway and Wantage Tramway (in 1878).

BG – Reproduction Broad Gauge (7ft 0¼ins) "Firefly" class locomotive.

Dia and **Lot** (Railcar No. 22) refer to the body style (carriage drawing – Diagram) and carriage works building series (Lot).

Year Built: u/c – under construction at Didcot Locomotive Works (Firefly).

Wheel Arrangement:

ST – Saddle Tank locomotive

T – (Side) Tank locomotive

PT – Pannier Tank Locomotive

WT – Well Tank Locomotive

4w-4w – carried on two powered four-wheeled bogies

DM – Diesel Mechanical Locomotive

DE – Diesel Electric Locomotive

Withdrawn:

IN – in various Industrial Use, 1934-1968

SC – in Industrial Use for Stephenson Clarke, 1963-1969

CW – worked at Corrall's coal wharfs Poole and Southampton, 1949-1969

MA – worked at Mountain Ash and Penrikyber collieries 1914-1969

WT – withdrawn from Wantage Tramway 1945. Preserved by GWR.

NC – Owned and used by National Coal Board, 1957-1978.

GWS Collection:

SM – Owned by Science Museum. On loan to GWS from 1996.

KE – Owned by 6024 Preservation Society (acquired 1973).

NR – Owned by National Railway Museum. On loan to GWS from 1969.

PO – Privately Owned.

Preservation:

LL – To be rebuilt as 2900 (Saint) class locomotive No. 2999 Lady of Legend.

In the lists of coaching stock and goods wagons the 'Diagram' is the number of the official Swindon drawing relating to the vehicle and the 'Lot No.' is the order number issued at Swindon for its construction.

COACHING STOCK

92 Churchward Auto Trailer. Built 1912 Diagram U Lot 1198

111 Collett Passenger Brake Van. Built 1934 Diagram K41 Lot 1512

190 Collett Auto Trailer. Built 1933 Diagram A30 Lot 1480

212 Collett Auto Trailer. Converted 1936 Diagram A26 Lot 1542 (originally Steam Railmotor 93. Built 1908 Diagram R Lot 1142)

231 Hawksworth Auto Trailer. Built 1951 (BR) Diagram A38 Lot 1736

290 Dean 4-wheel Composite 1st/2nd. Built 1902 Diagram U4 Lot 990

416 Dean 4-wheel Brake Third. Built 1891 Diagram T49 Lot 582

484 Churchward "Monster" Carriage Truck. Built 1913 Diagram P18 Lot 1223

536 Collett Third. Built 1940 Diagram C77 Lot 1623

565 Churchward "Python" Covered Carriage Truck. Built 1914 Diagram P19 Lot 1238

814 Collett Travelling Post Office Brake Stowage Van. Built 1940 Diagram L23 Lot 1666

933 Dean Passenger Brake Van. Built 1898 Diagram K14 Lot 883

975 Dean 4-wheel Third. Built 1902 Diagram S9 Lot 992

1111 Collett Third. Built 1938 Diagram C77 Lot 1593

1159 Medical Officers' Coach. Converted 1945 Diagram M33 Lot 1481 (originally Churchward Passenger Brake Van - Toplight. Built 1925 Diagram K36 Lot 1344)

1184 Collett Passenger Brake Van. Built 1930 Diagram K40 Lot 1413

1289 Collett Excursion Third. Built 1937 Diagram C74 Lot 1575

1357 Dean Third - Clerestory. Built 1903 Diagram C22 Lot 1038

1941 Dean Third - Clerestory. Built 1901 Diagram C10 Lot 962

2202 Hawksworth Brake Third. Built 1950 (BR) Diagram D133 Lot 1732

2511 Dean 6-wheel Family Saloon. Built 1894 Diagram G20 Lot 740

2796 Churchward "Siphon G" Bogie Milk Churn Van. Built 1937 Diagram O33 Lot 1578

3299 Churchward Third - Dreadnought. Built 1905 Diagram C24 Lot 1098

3755 Churchward non-corridor Brake Third - City stock. Built 1921 Diagram D62 Lot 1275

3756 Churchward non-corridor Brake Third - City stock. Built 1921 Diagram D62 Lot 1275

4553 Collett Third - Bow ended. Built 1925 Diagram C54 Lot 1352

5085 Collett Third - Bow ended. Built 1928 Diagram C54 Lot 1383

5787 Collett Brake Third. Built 1933 Diagram D116 Lot 1490

5952 Collett All Third. Built 1935 Diagram C67 Lot 1527

6824 Dean 6-wheel Tri-composite. Built 1887 Diagram U29 Lot 370 (convertable coach - originally built for Broad Gauge)

7285 Collett Composite. Built 1941 Diagram E162 Lot 1639

7313 Collett Composite. Built 1940 Diagram E158 Lot 1621

7371 Collett Brake Composite. Built 1941 Diagram 159 Lot 1640

7372 Hawksworth Brake Composite. Built 1948 (BR) Diagram E164 Lot 1690

7976 Collett Brake Composite. Built 1923 Diagram E114 Lot 1323

9002 Collett Special Saloon. Built 1940 Diagram G62 Lot 1626

9083 Hawksworth First Sleeping Car. Built 1951 (BR) Diagram J18 Lot 1702

9112 Collett Super Saloon "Queen Mary". Built 1932 Diagram G60 Lot 1471

9113 Collett Super Saloon "Prince of Wales". Built 1932 Diagram G61 Lot 1471

9118 Collett Super Saloon Kitchen "Princess Elizabeth". Converted 1935 Diagram H46 (originally Super Saloon. Built 1932 Diagram G61 Lot 1471)

9520 Dean Composite Diner-Clerestory. Built 1903 Diagram H7 Lot 1011 (carried on chassis of 3655, Churchward Third, Built 1921)

9635 Collett First Diner - Centenary Stock. Built 1935 Diagram H43 Lot 1540

GOODS WAGONS – GWR STOCK

101 6-wheel Drinking Water Tank Wagon - 3,000 gals. Built 1946 Diagram DD6 Lot 1555

263 Signal & Telegraph Department Mess Van. Converted 1952 (BR) (originally 25 ton Brake Van 56867. Built 1905 Diagram AA2 Lot 477)

752 Special Cattle Van. Built 1952 (BR Ashford) Diagram W17 Lot 1774

2356 "Fruit" Van. Built 1892 Diagram Y2 Lot 638

2671 "Bloater" Fish Van. Built 1926 Diagram S10 Lot 1356c

2862 "Fruit C" Passenger Fruit Van. Built 1938 Diagram Y9 Lot 1634c

3030 "Rotank" Flat Wagon to carry road tank trailer. Built 1947 Diagram O58 Lot 1715

10153 Open Wagon, 7 plank. Built for Taff Vale Railway.

11152 "Iron Mink" iron-bodied van. Built 1900 Diagram V6 Lot 217 (Restored as 47305 in wartime salvage campaign livery)

19818 "Open A" Open Wagon, 5 plank. Built 1918 Diagram O11 Lot 834

32337 ⎫ "Mite D" Twin Articulated Single Bolster Wagons. Built 1881
32338 ⎭ Diagram J9 Lot 220

41723 "Coral A" Well Wagon to carry glass in crates. Built 1908 Diagram D2 Lot 583

41934 "Crocodile F" Bogie Well Wagon. Built 1908 Diagram C12 Lot 594

42193 "Hydra D" Well Wagon. Built 1917 Diagram G22 Lot 745 (On loan from National Railway Museum)

42239 "Grain" Convertible Hopper Van. Built 1927 Diagram V20 Lot 1006

42271 "Loriot L" Well Wagon. Built 1934 Diagram G13 Lot 1142

43949 Tank Wagon - 3108 gals oil/creosote etc. Built 1911 Diagram DD3 Lot 286

56100 "Toad" 14 (later 16) ton Brake Van. Built 1895 Diagram AA3 Lot 38

63066 Loco Coal Wagon, steel body. Built 1946 Diagram N34 Lot 1480

68684 "Toad" 20 ton Brake Van. Built 1924 Diagram AA15 Lot 910

70335 "Macaw B" Bogie Bolster Wagon. Built 1939 Diagram J28 Lot 1372

79933 "Tevan" Special Traffics Van. Converted 1938 Diagram V31 (originally "Mica B" Meat Van. Built 1922 Diagram X7 Lot 890)

80668 Ballast Wagon, steel body (10 ton). Built 1936 Diagram P15 Lot 1215

80789 Ballast Wagon, steel body (20 ton). Built 1937 Diagram P17 Lot 1243

92943 China Clay Wagon - 5 plank. Built 1913 Diagram O13 Lot 750

94835 "Open C" Open Wagon, 4 plank. Built 1920 Diagram O19 Lot 844

100377 Shunters Truck. Converted 1953 (originally "Mink A" Van. Built 1923 Diagram V14 Lot 882)

100682 Wagon for Concrete Sleepers. Built 1939 Diagram T12 Lot 1313*

101720 "Mink A" Van. Built 1924 Diagram V14 Lot 911

101836 "Mink A" Van. Built 1925 Diagram V14 Lot 911

105599 "Fruit B" Banana Van. Built 1929 Diagram Y7 Lot 1054

105742 "Mogo" Motor Car Van. Built 1936 Diagram G31 Lot 1224

105860 "Mica B" Meat Van. Built 1925 Diagram X8 Lot 921

112843 "Mink G" Express Freight Van. Built 1931 Diagram V22 Lot 1067

116954 "Asmo" Motor Car Van. Built 1930 Diagram G26 Lot 1059

117993 "Open" Open Wagon, 5 plank. Built 1930 Diagram O29 Lot 1043

145428 "Van". Built 1944 Diagram V34 Lot 1431

146366 "Van", plywood body. Built 1948 (BR) Diagram V38 Lot 1525

950592 "Toad" 20 ton Brake Van. Built 1950 (BR) Diagram AA23 Lot 2099

*100682 is fitted with pipes for air brakes and is used to carry stores and materials in and out of the Railway Centre, it carries main line Registration number GWS 91200.

c = Carriage Lot number

NON-GWR GOODS WAGONS

   1   Rectangular Tar Tank Wagon. Built 1898 by Charles Roberts & Co. (Restored as Smith & Forrest, Manchester. No. 1)

  18   Open Wagon, 5 plank. Built 1927. (Restored as John North, Abingdon, No. 18)

 745   Oil Tank Wagon. Built 1912 by Hurst Nelson, Motherwell. (Restored as Royal Daylight, No. 745)

S4409   6-wheel Milk Tank Wagon (Express Dairies). Built by Southern Railway.

SERVICE VEHICLES

 5267   OJA 21 ton Coal Wagon (formerly BR B15024). Built 1956

 5268   OJA 21 ton Coal Wagon (formerly BR B15029). Built 1956

10509   Dormitory Coach, formerly BR Mark lll Sleeping Car. Built 1981 Lot 30960

15565   Dormitory Coach, formerly BR Mark I Composite. Built 1955 Lot 30135

15577   Dormitory Coach, formerly BR Mark I Composite. Built 1955 Lot 30135

34671   Railtour Support Coach - Main line Registration: GWS 99512. BR Mark I Brake Second. Built 1955 Lot 30156

80224   Railtour Support Coach - BR Mark I NNX Courier Vehicle - formerly Brake Second 35291. Built 1960 Lot 30573

100682   Stores Wagon - Main line Registration GWS 91200. Formerly Concrete Sleeper Wagon, see GWR Goods Wagon list above.

CRANES

Hand Crane and Match Truck

 205   Hand Crane, built 1894, to order H2827
           Match Truck, built 1930 to order H1665

Steam Cranes

RS 1054   50 ton Breakdown Crane, built 1930 by Cowans Sheldon for London Midland & Scottish Railway.

23059   5 ton Shunting Crane, built 1954 by Thomas Smith and Sons (Rodley) Ltd., Leeds

Diesel Crane

CD 24   5 ton Shunting Crane, built 1949 by Thomas Smith and Sons (Rodley) Ltd., Leeds. Works No. 18820

BREAKDOWN TRAIN VEHICLES

   1   Tool Van. Built 1908 Lot 570
  47   Riding Van. Built 1908 Lot 580
  56   Riding Van. Built 1908 Lot 571
 135   Tool Van. Built 1908 Lot 579

The 5 ton steam crane in action.

DIDCOT RAILWAY CENTRE
General Plan

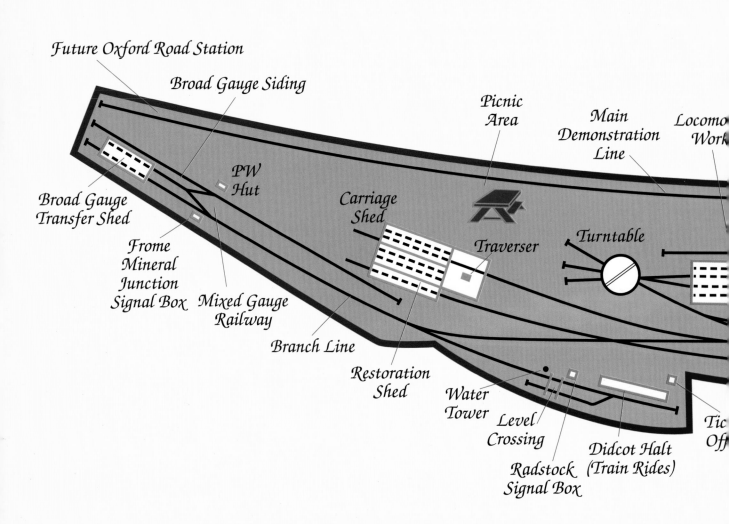

Future Oxford Road Station

Broad Gauge Siding

Picnic Area

Main Demonstration Line

Locomo Work

PW Hut

Broad Gauge Transfer Shed

Carriage Shed

Traverser

Turntable

Frome Mineral Junction Signal Box

Mixed Gauge Railway

Branch Line

Restoration Shed

Water Tower

Level Crossing

Radstock Signal Box

Didcot Halt (Train Rides)

Tic Off